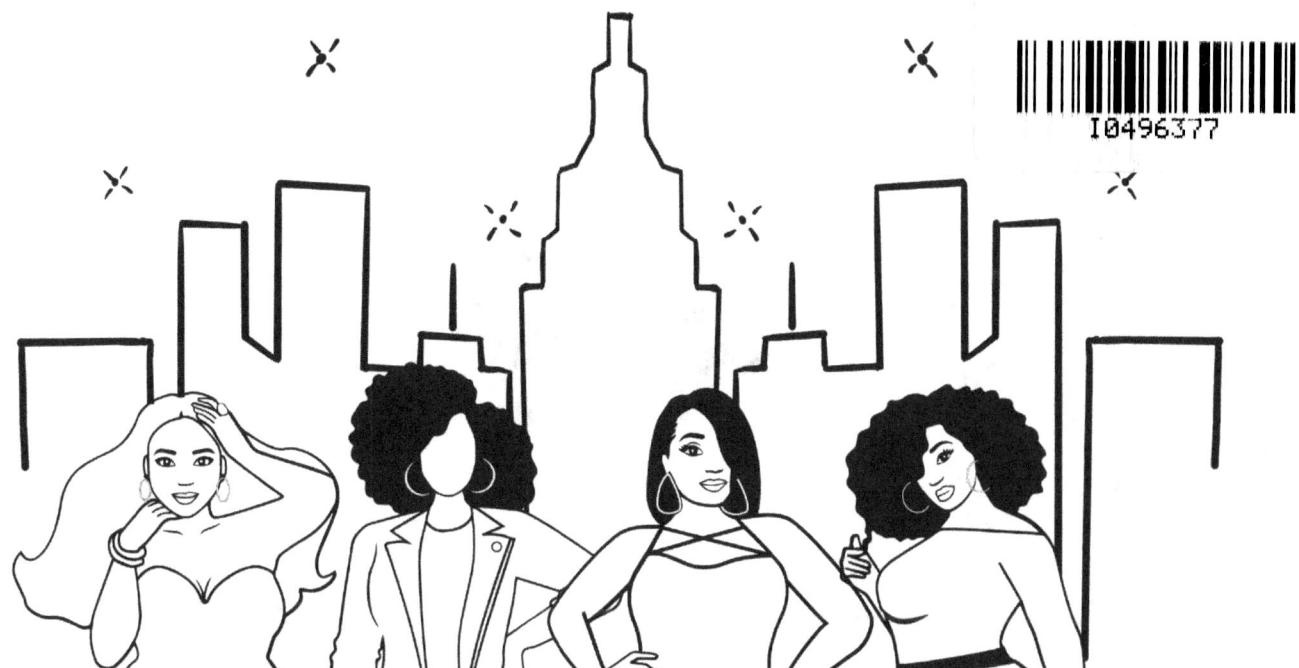

This Book Belongs To:

_____

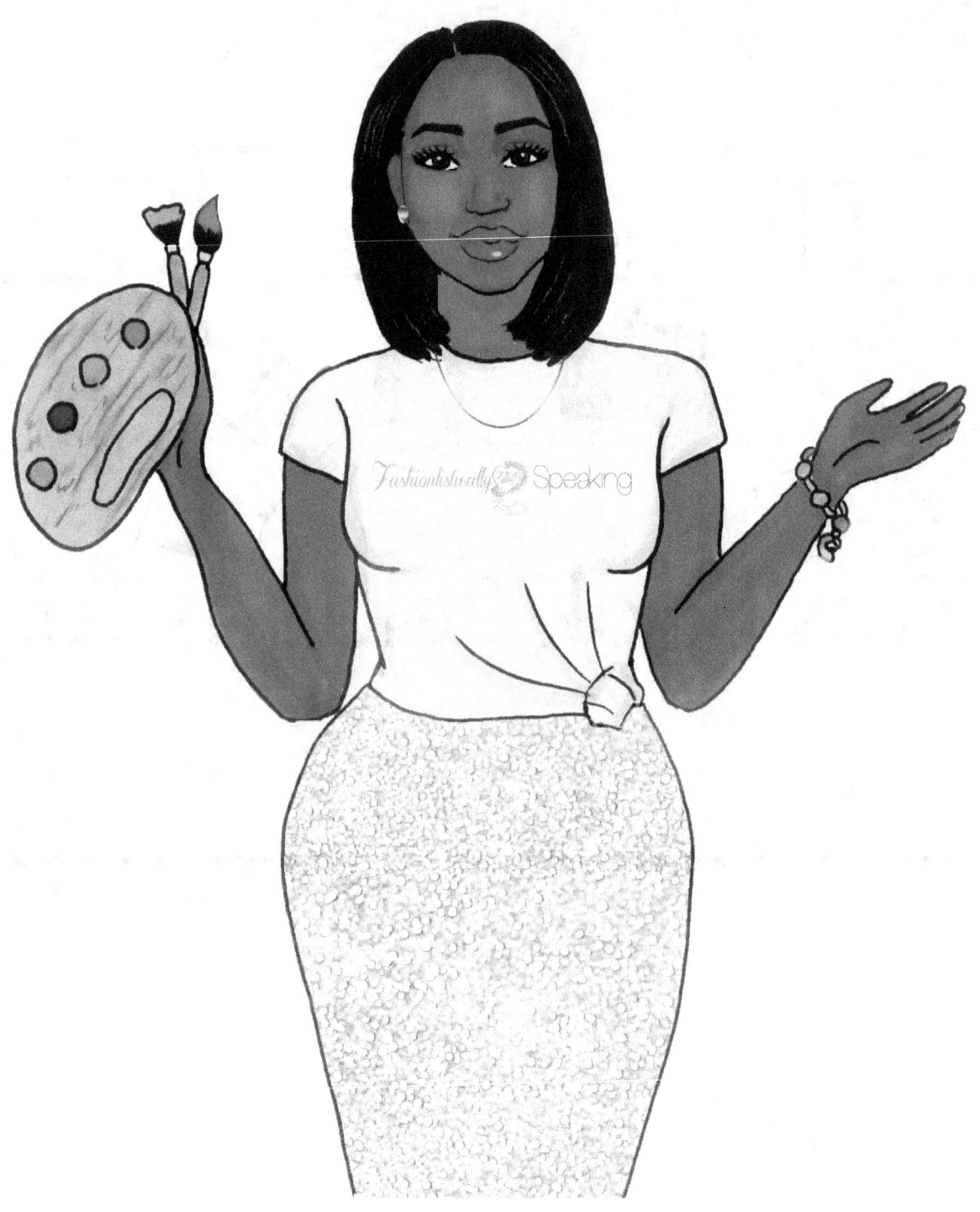

ISBN: 9798643596202

Copyright © 2020 by Crystal Caraway
All rights reserved. This book or any portion thereof
may not be reproduced or used in any manner whatsoever
without the express written permission of the publisher
except for the use of brief quotations in a book review.

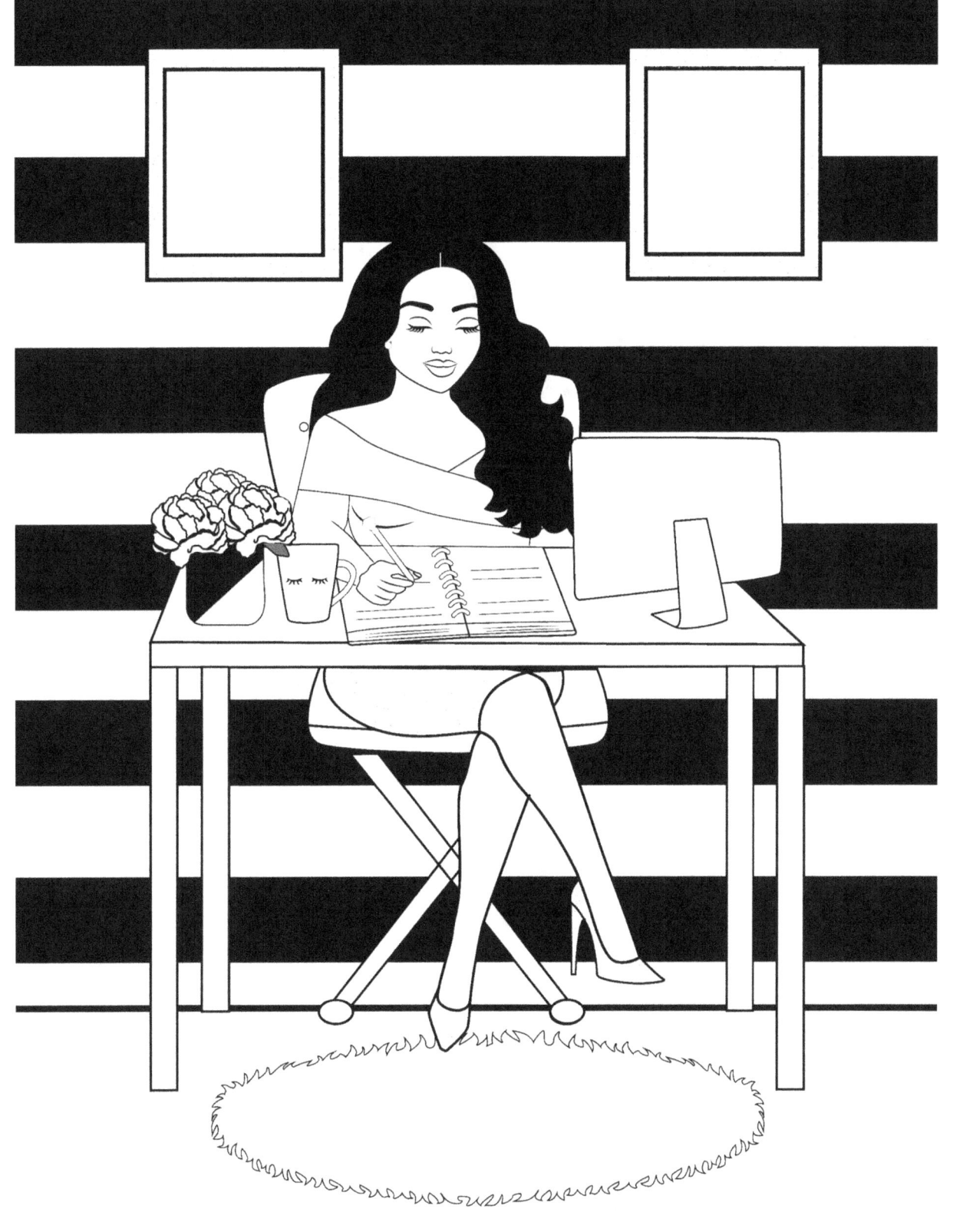

Fashionlistically Speaking

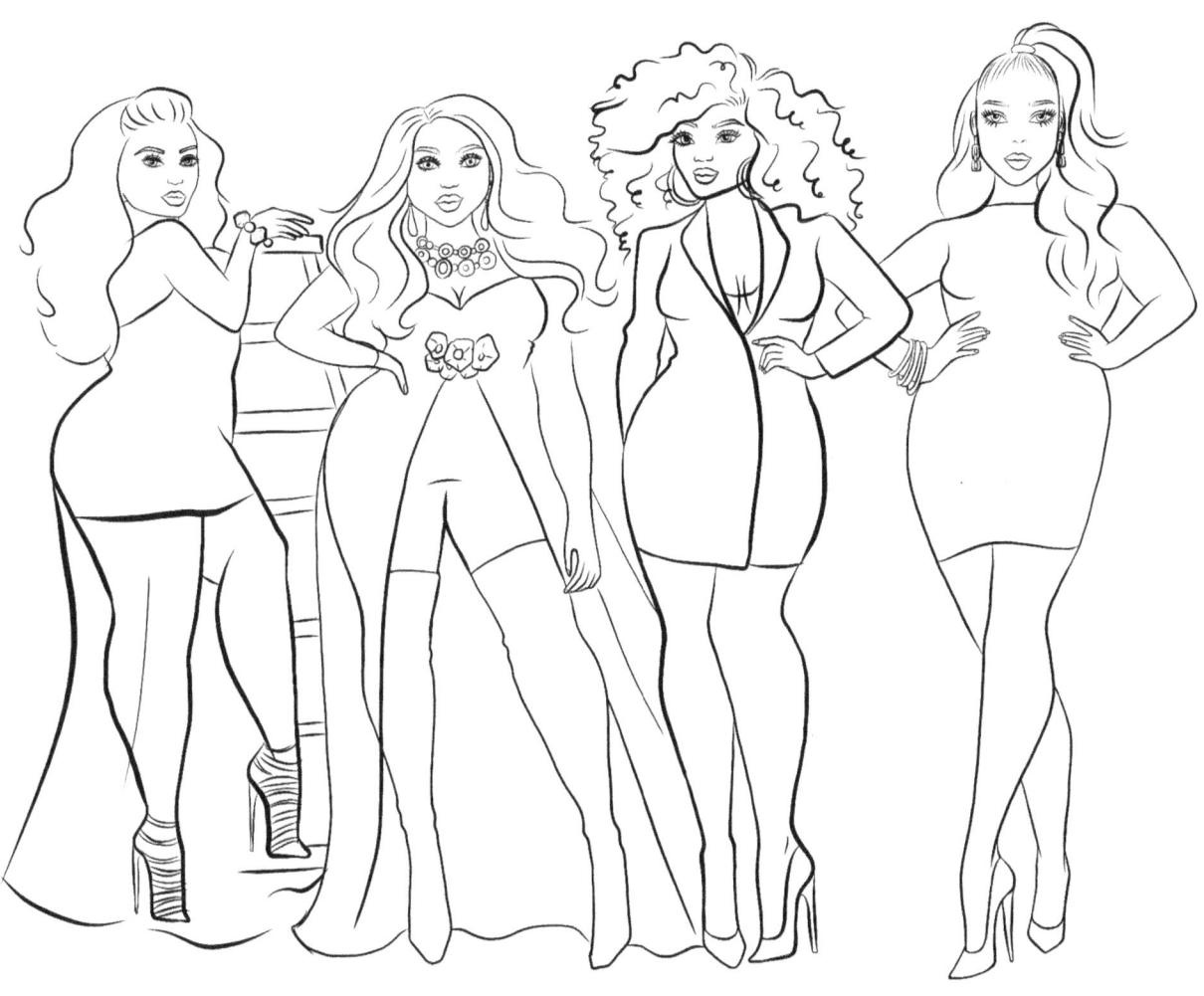

Fashionlistically Speaking

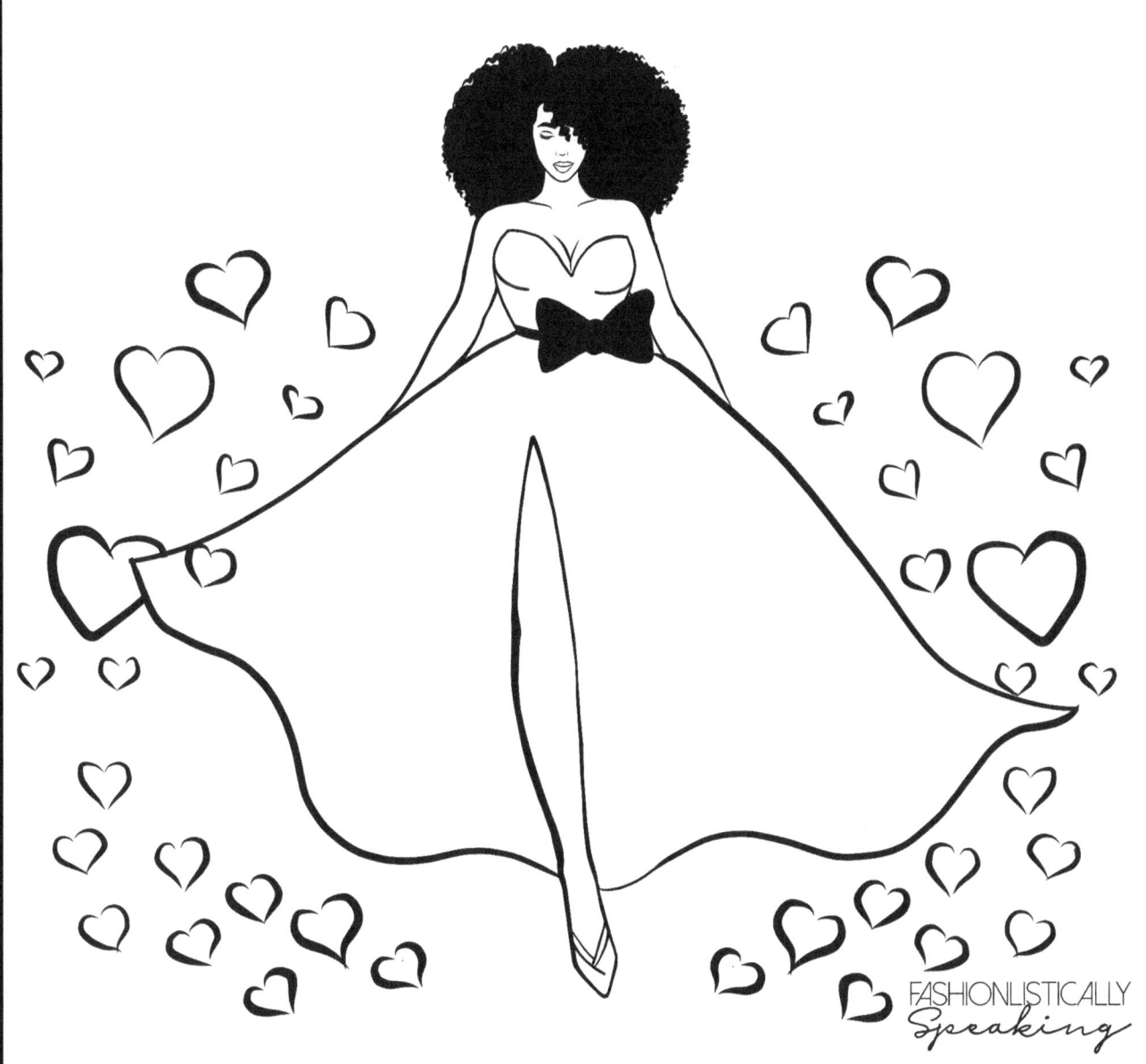

Fashionlistically Speaking

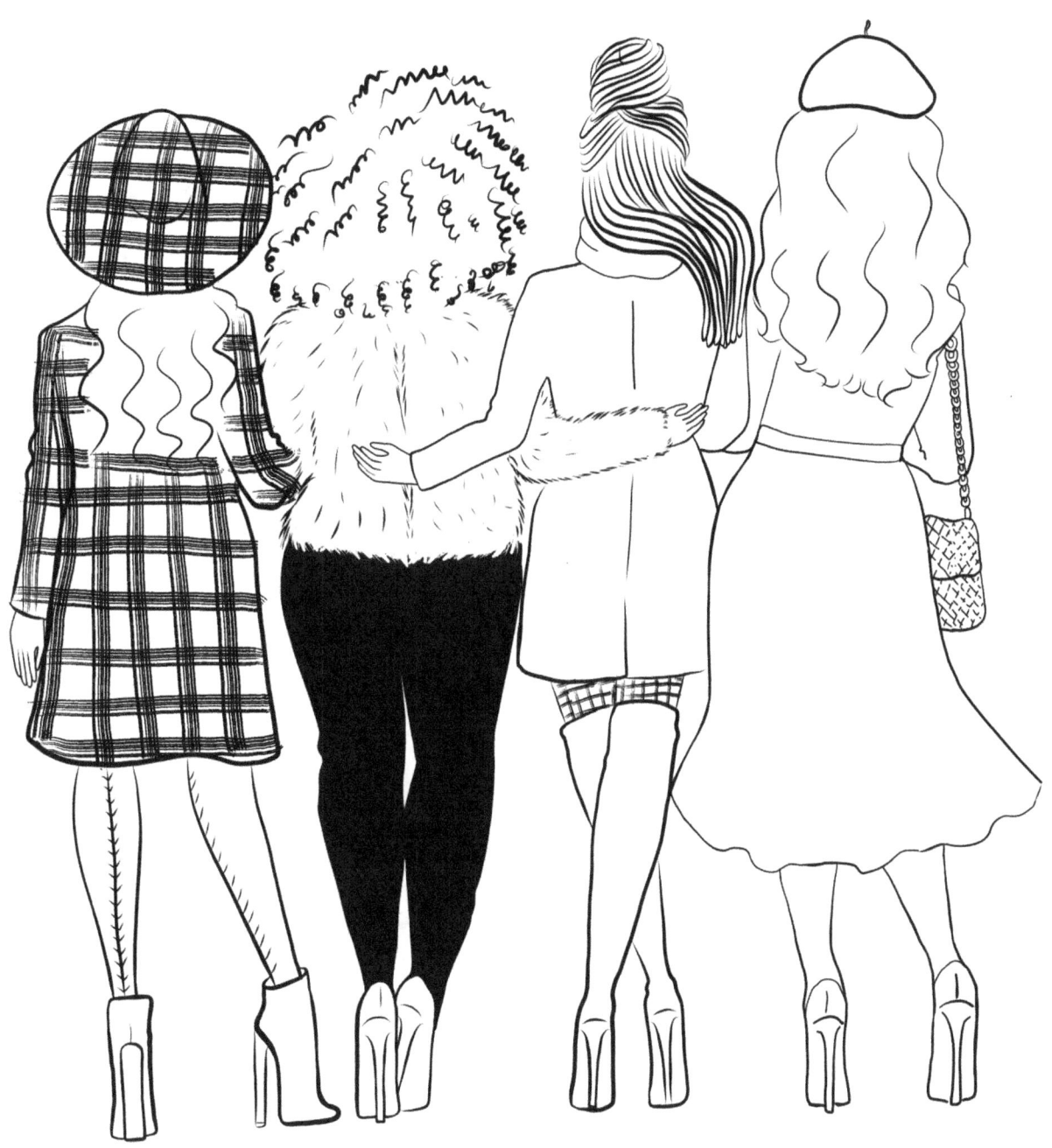

Fashionlistically Speaking

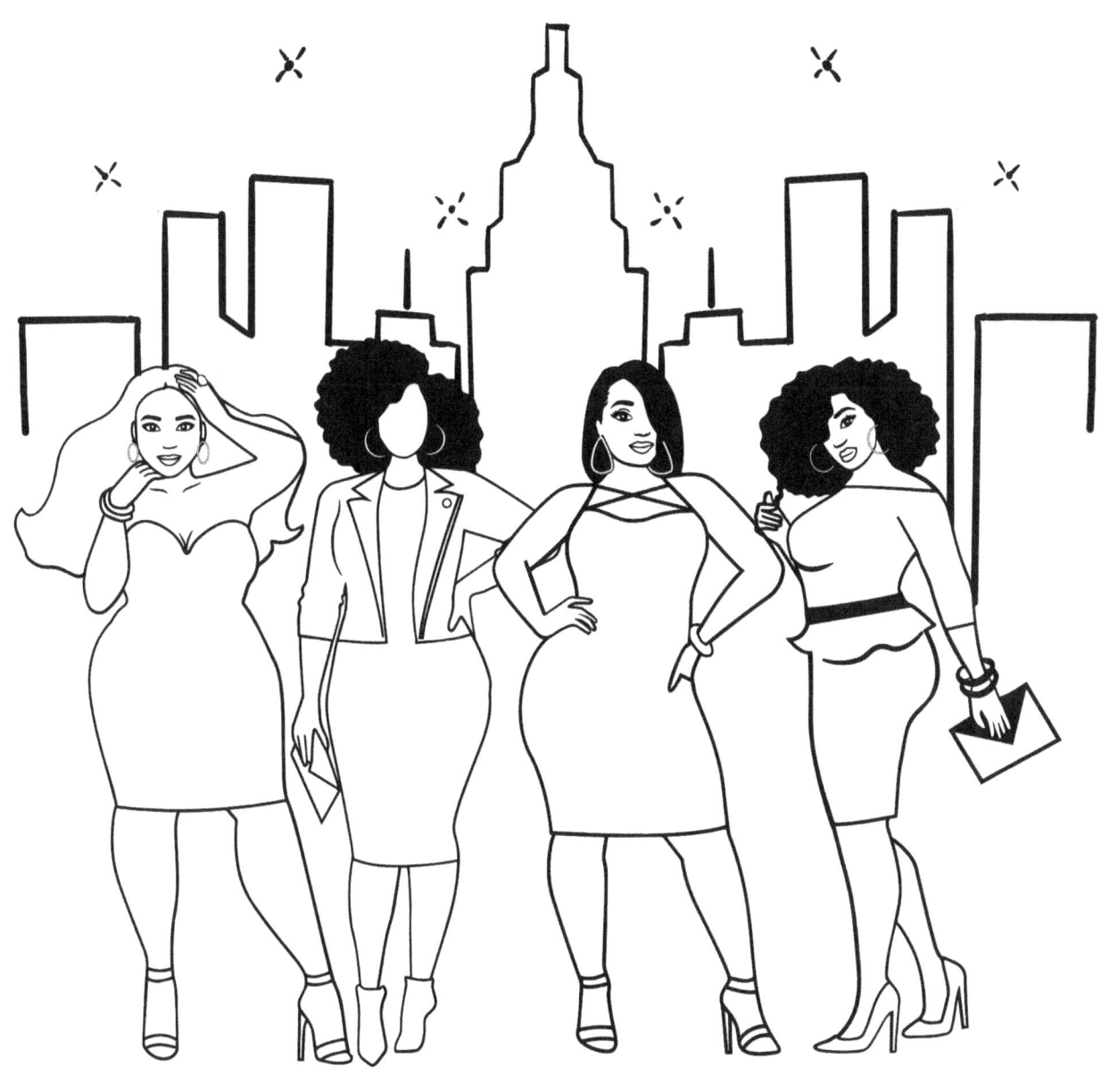

Fashionlistically Speaking

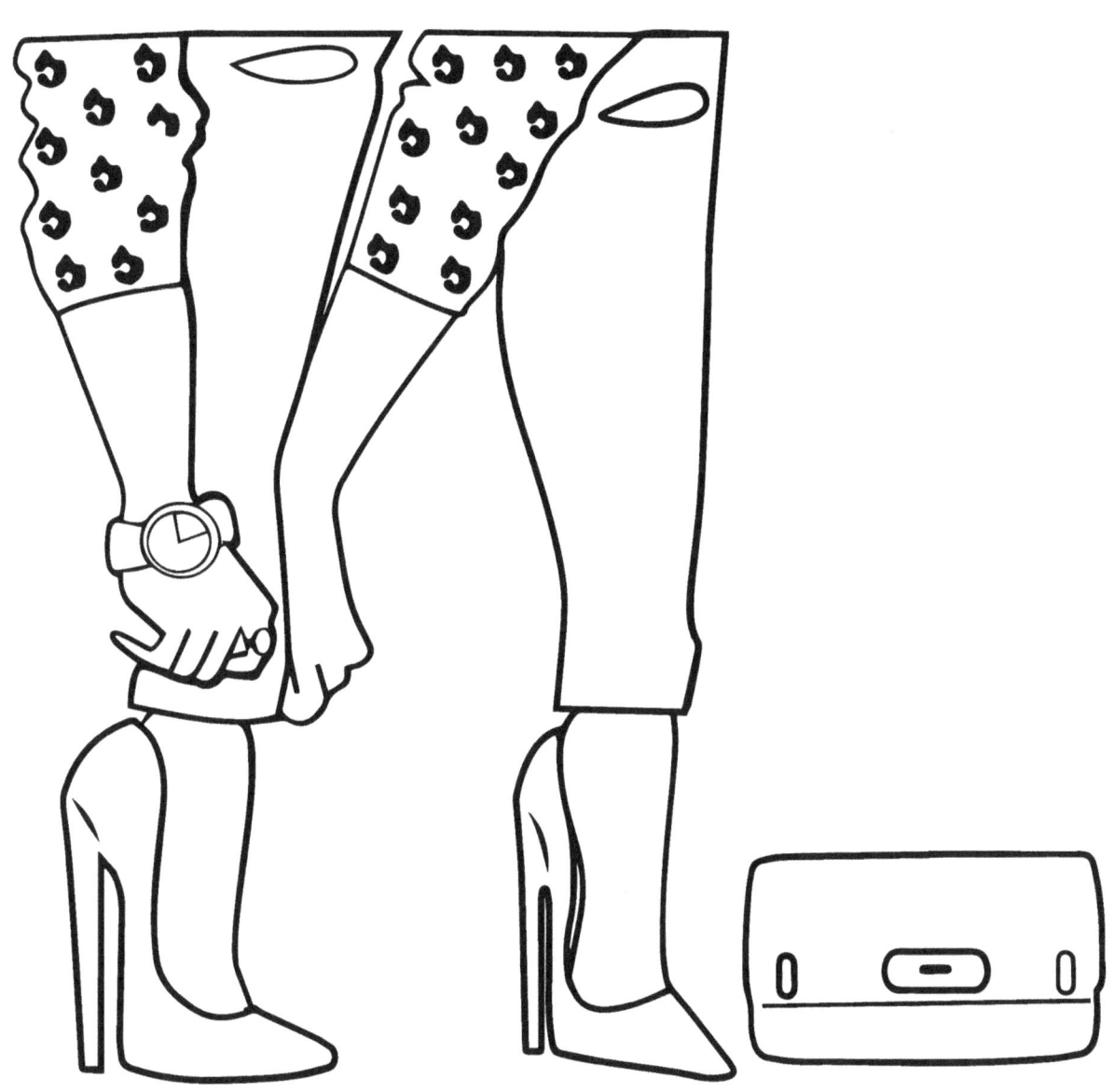

Fashionlistically Speaking

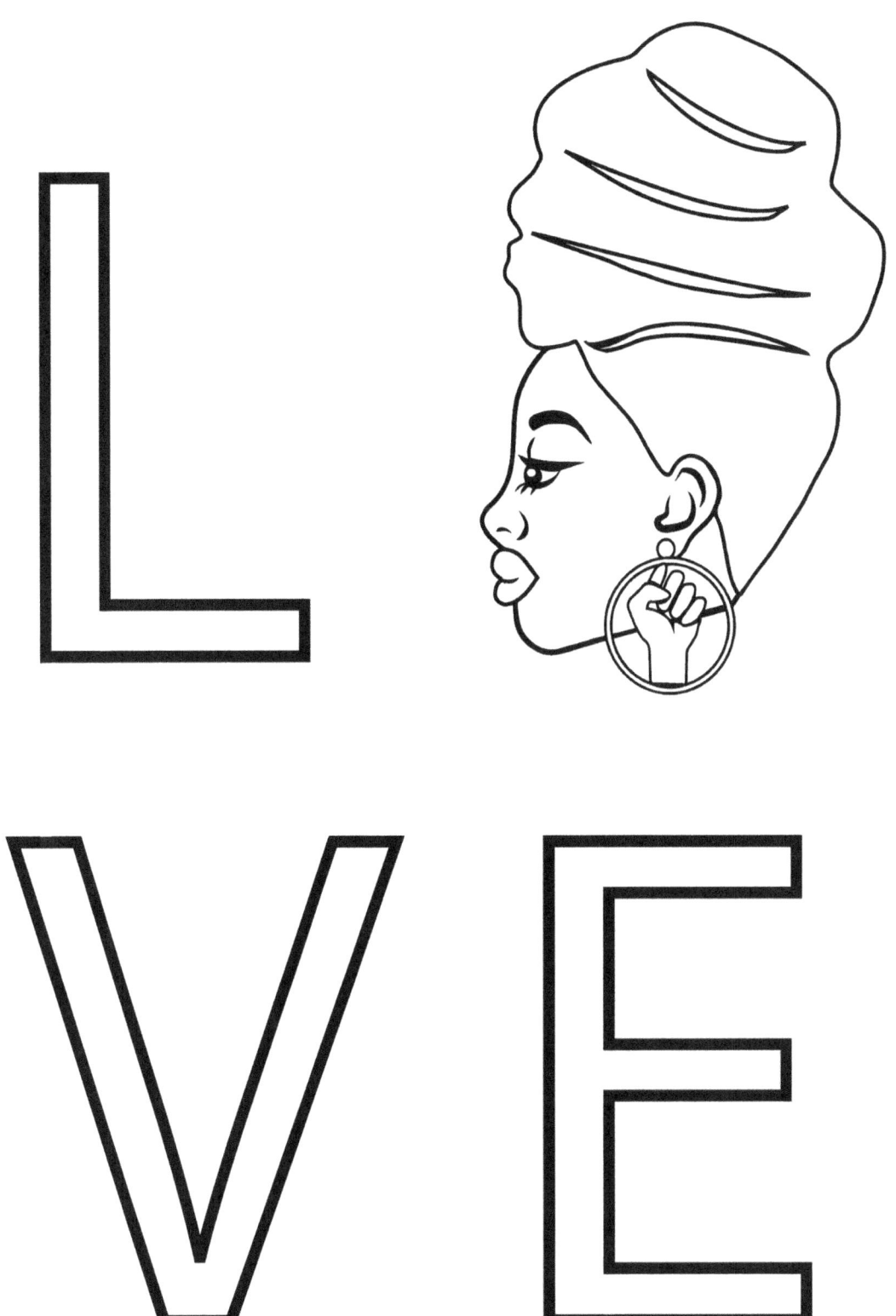

Fashionlistically Speaking

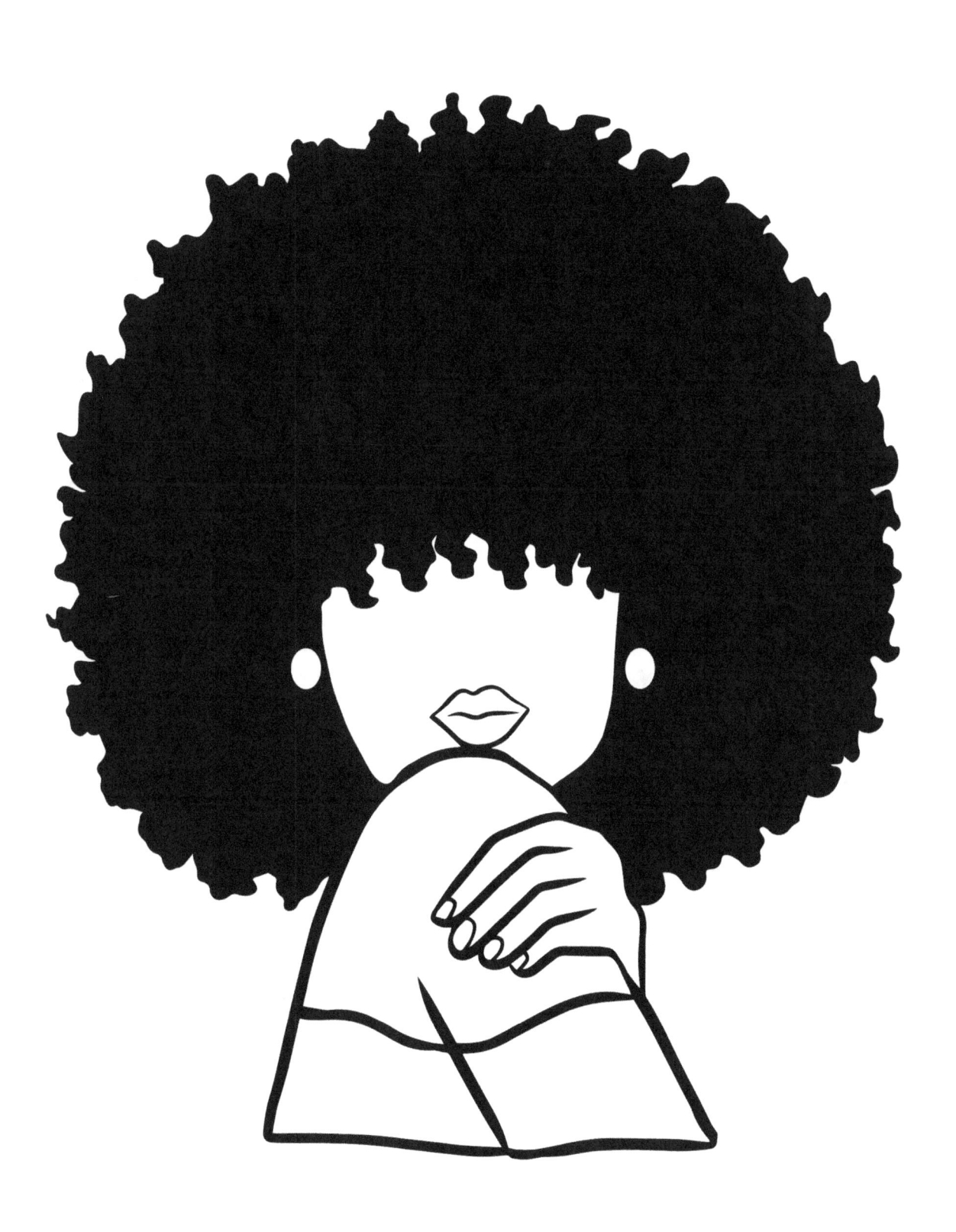

Fashionlistically Speaking

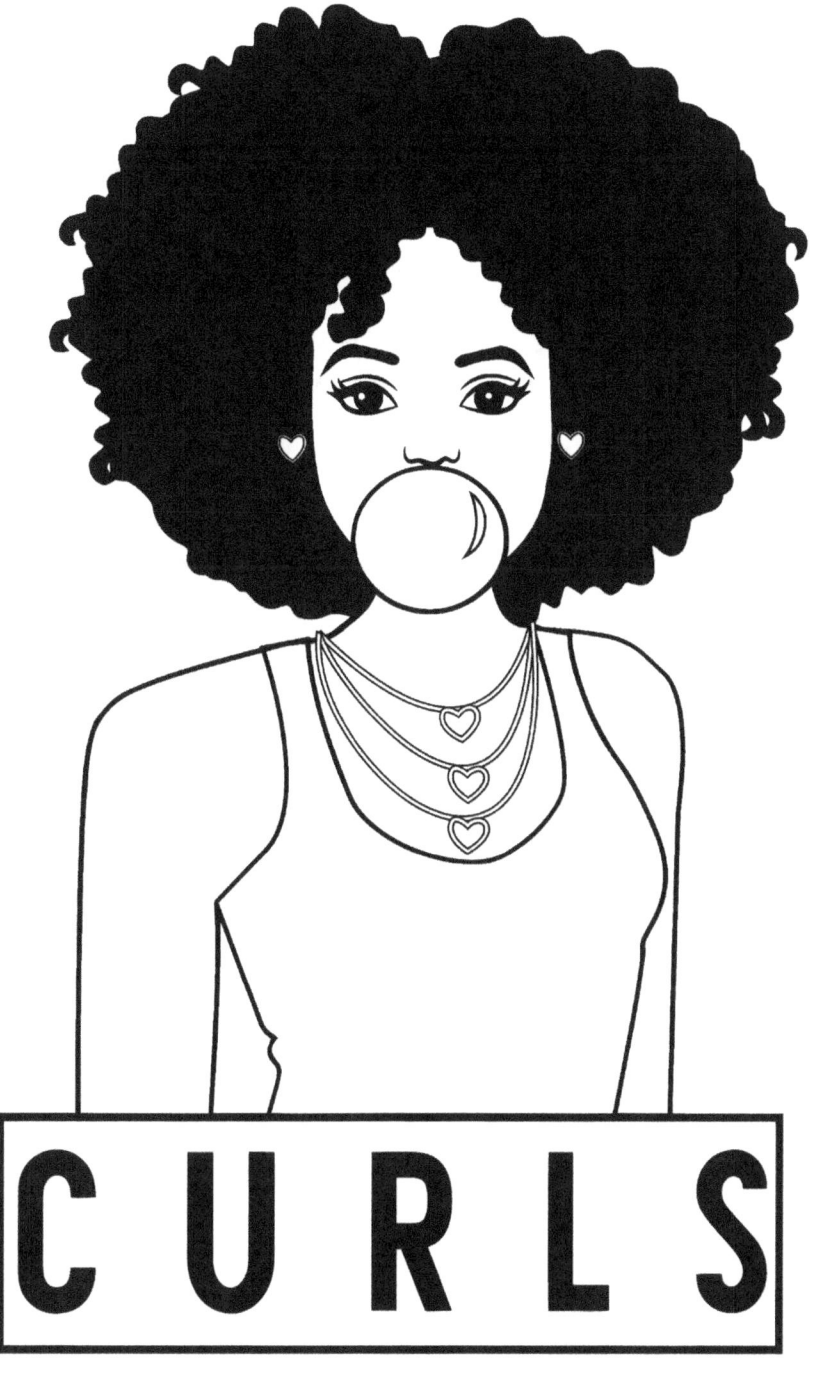

Fashionlistically Speaking

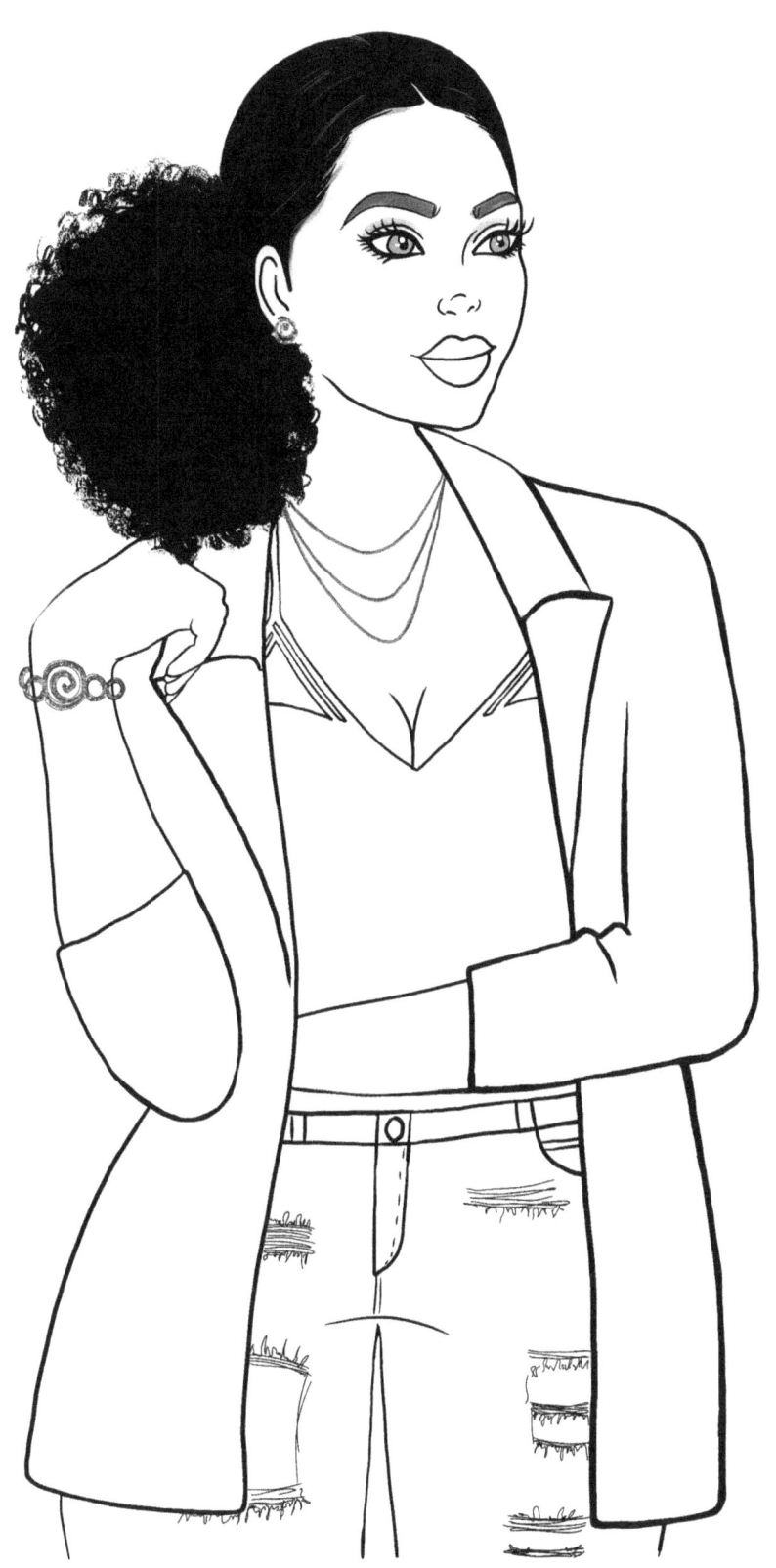

Fashionlistically Speaking

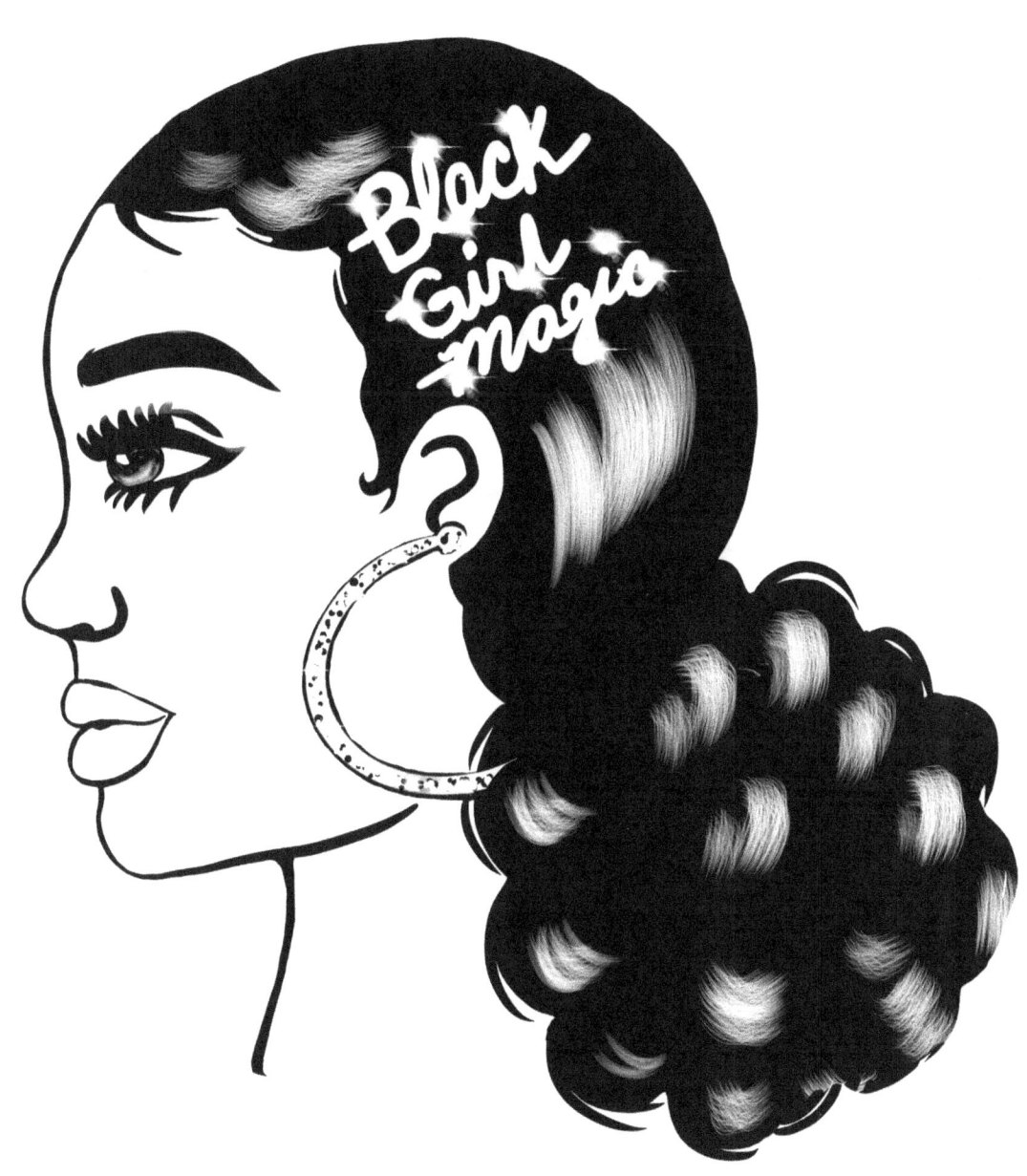

Fashionlistically Speaking

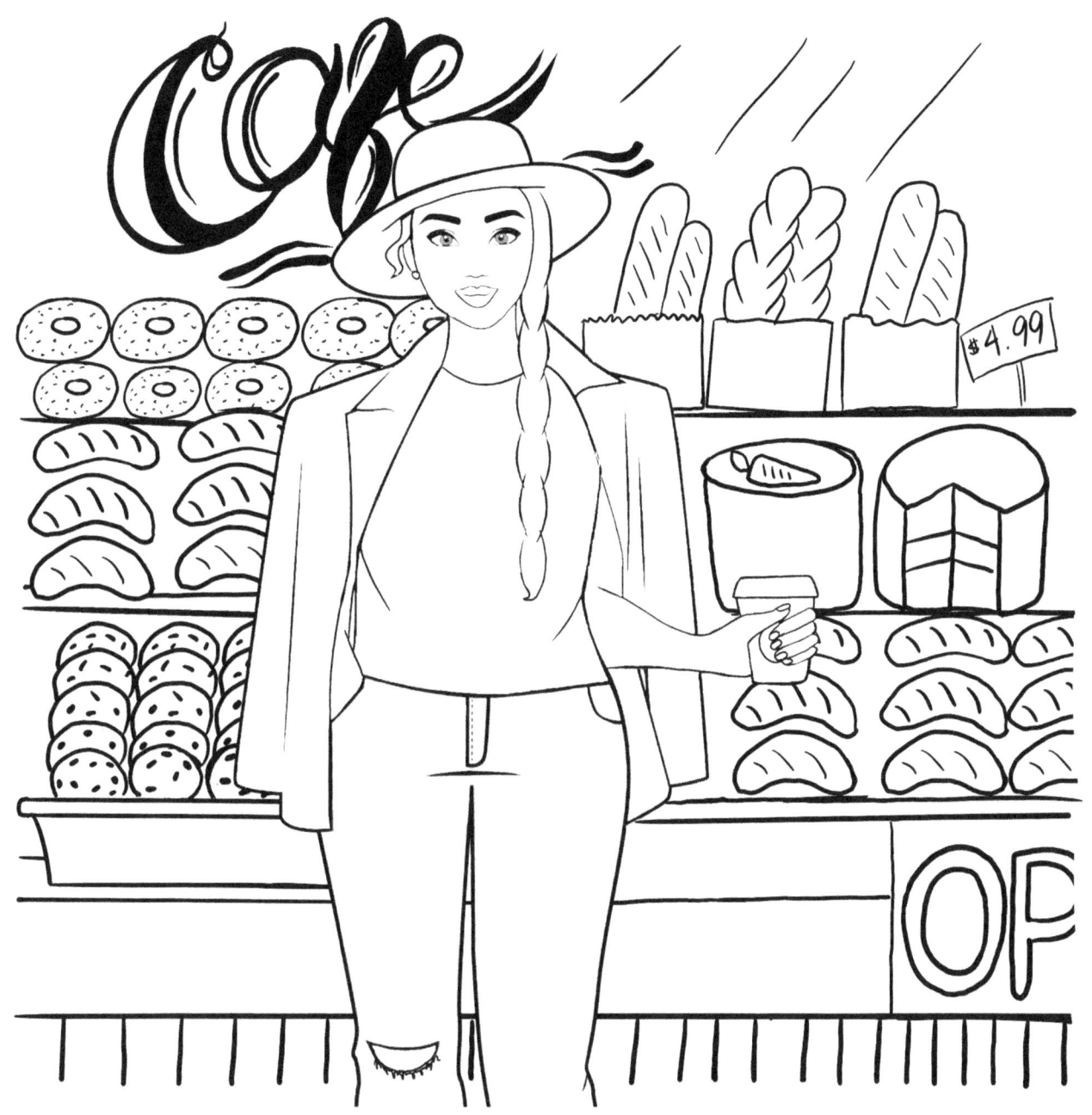

Fashionlistically Speaking

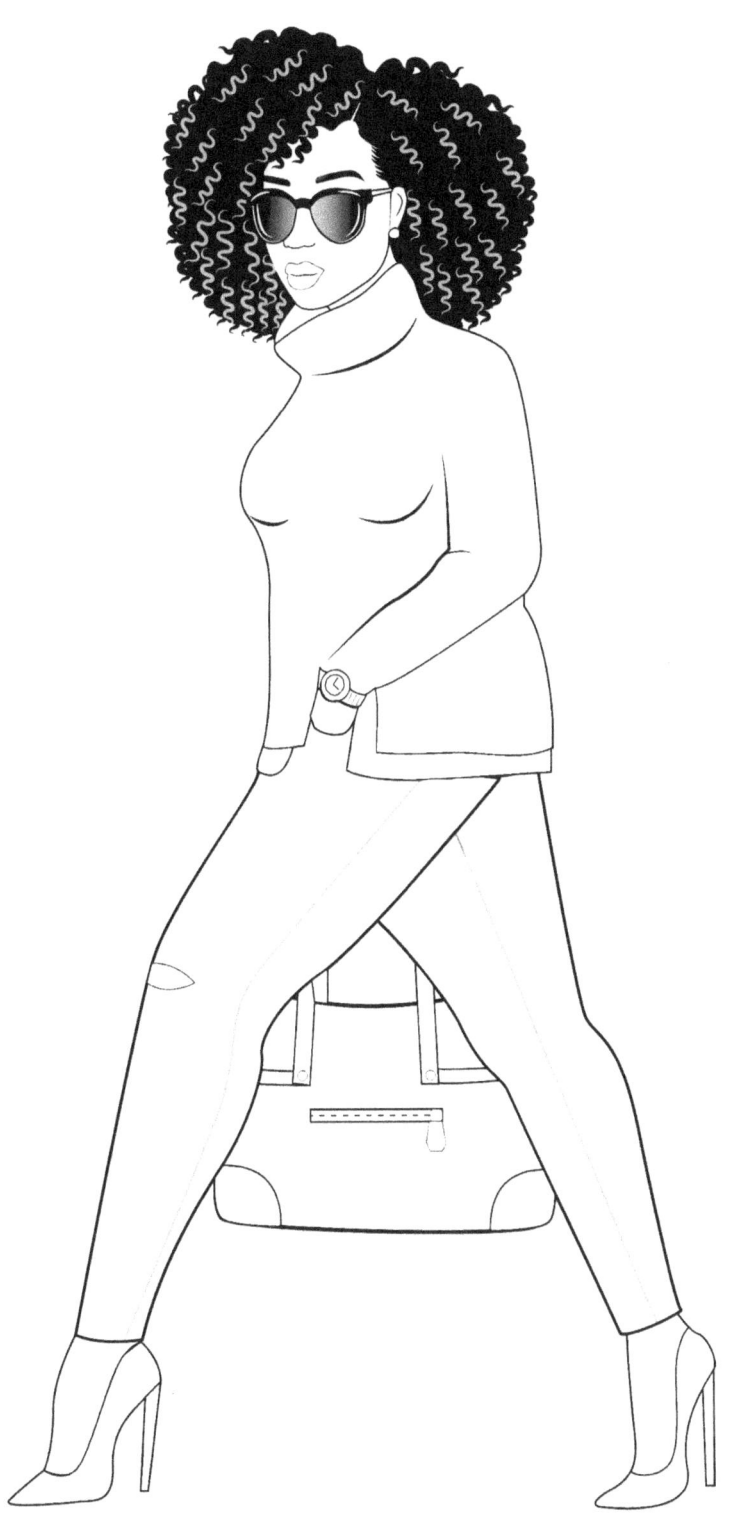

Fashionlistically Speaking

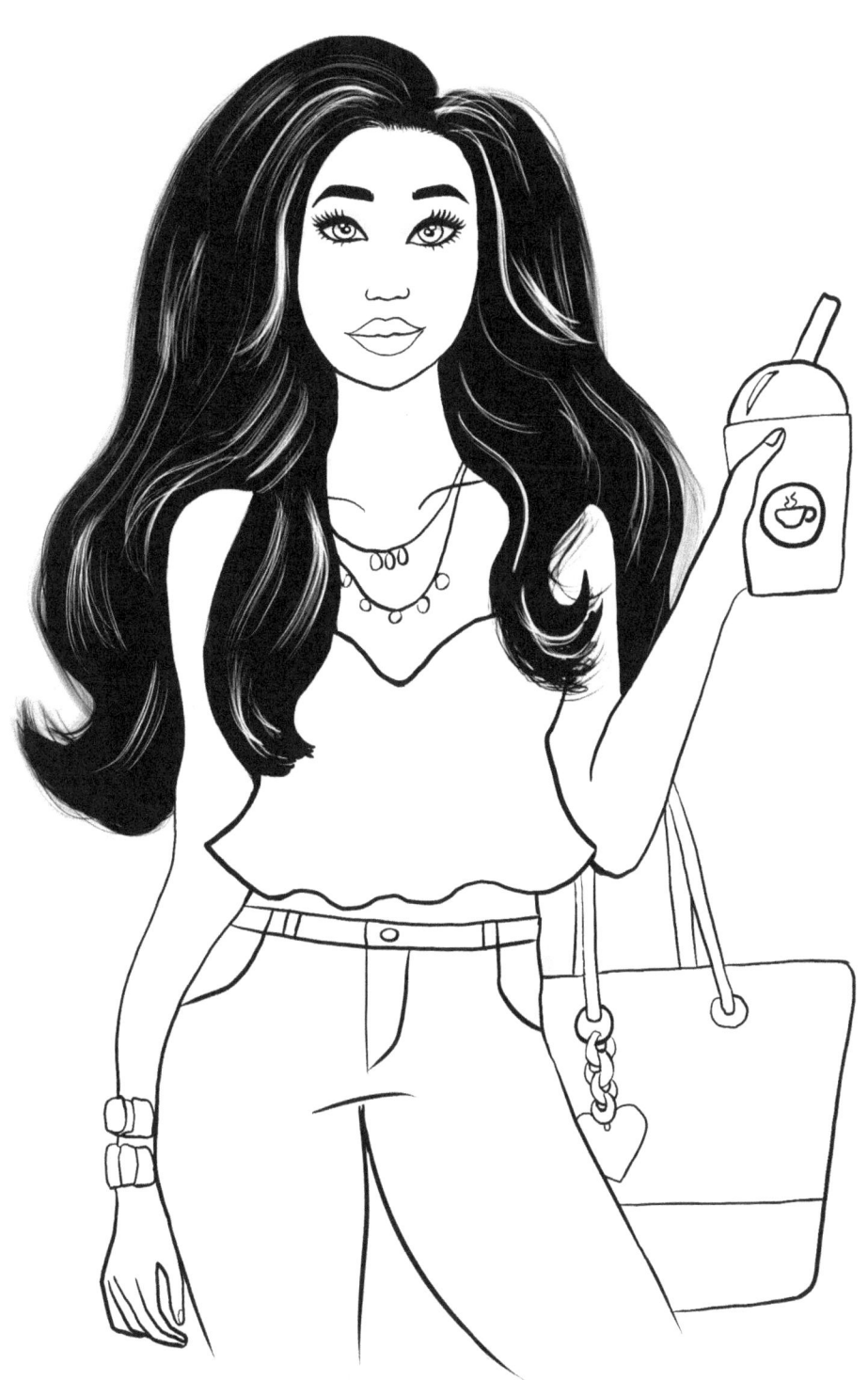

Fashionlistically Speaking

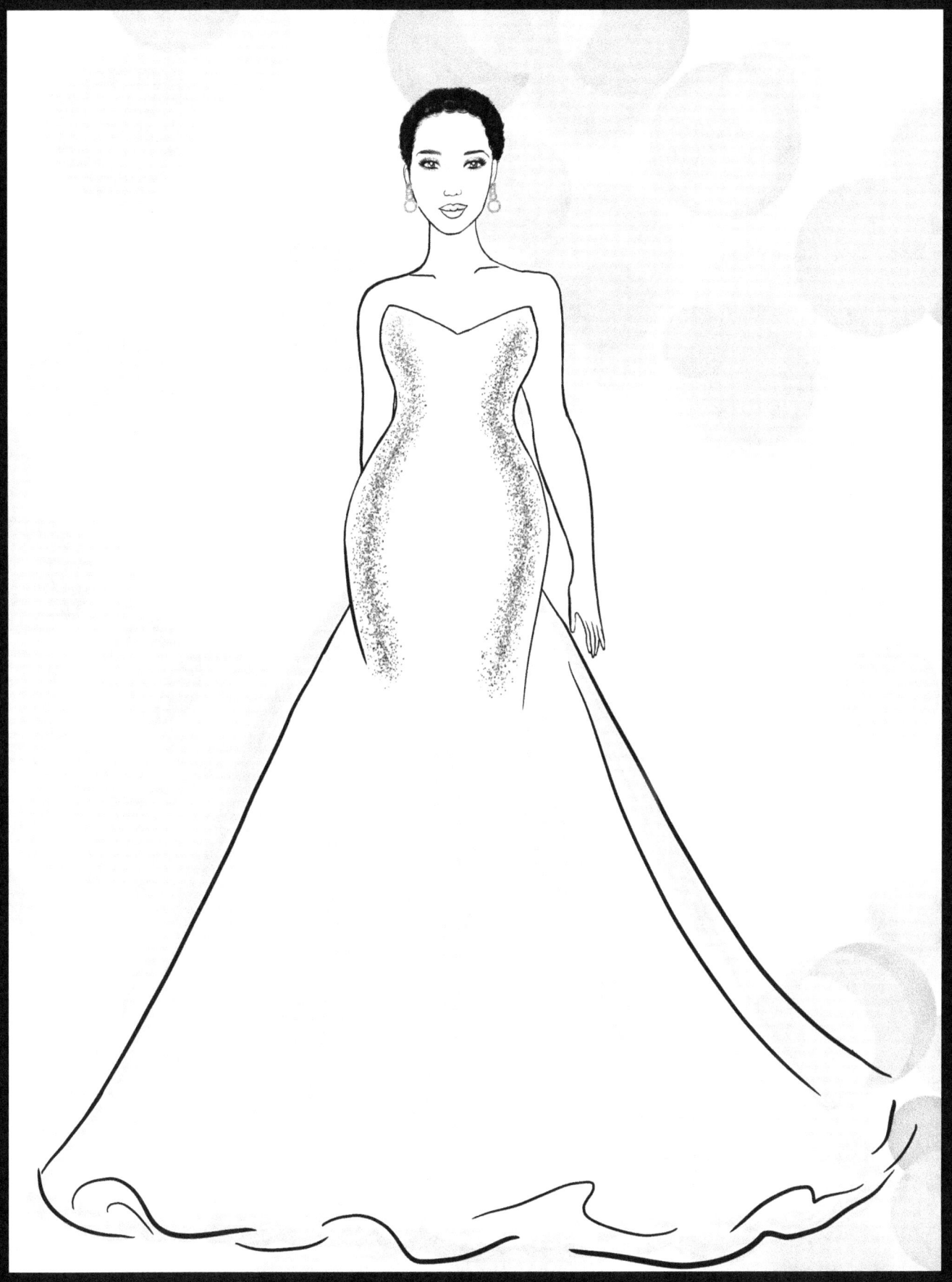

Fashionlistically Speaking

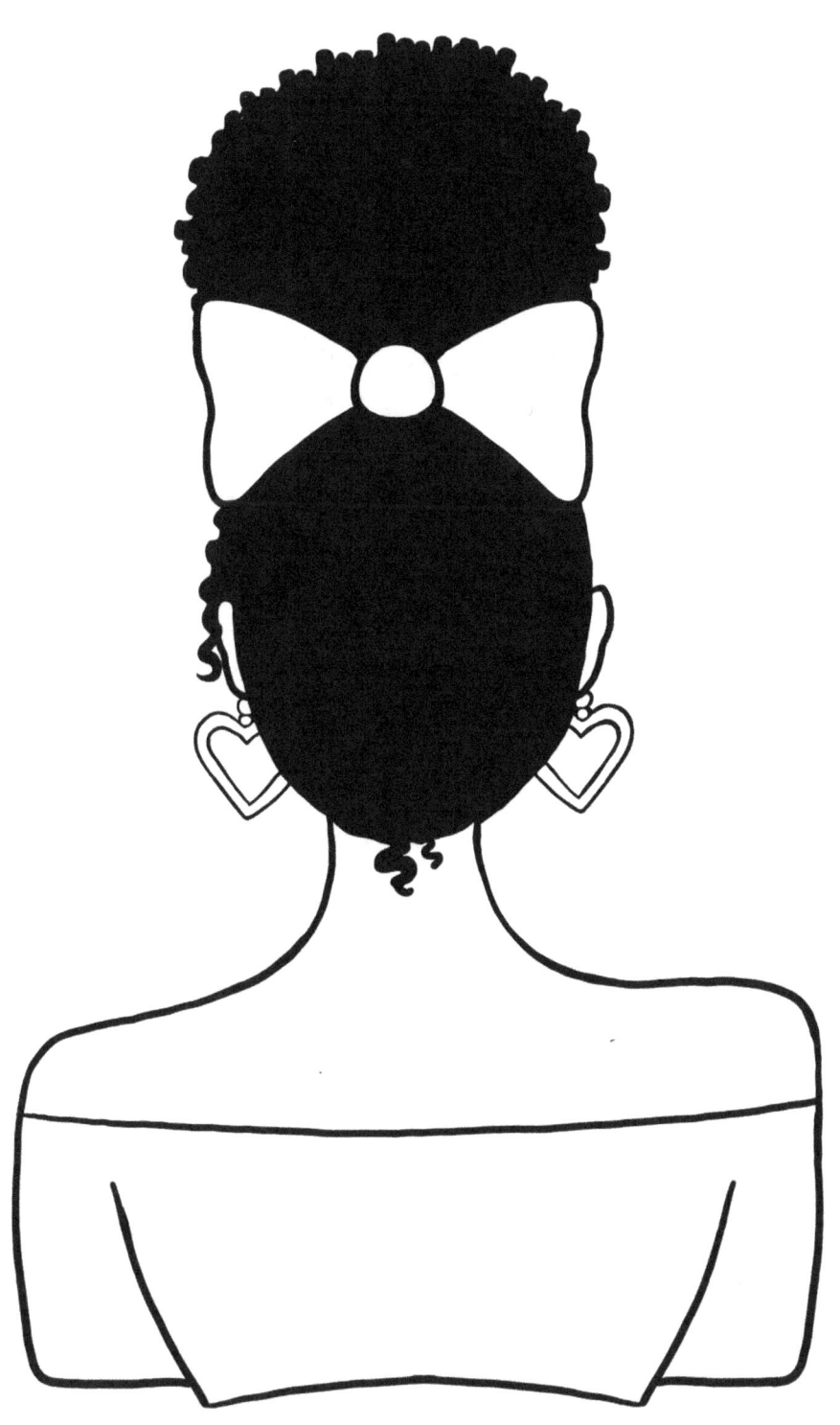

Fashionlistically Speaking

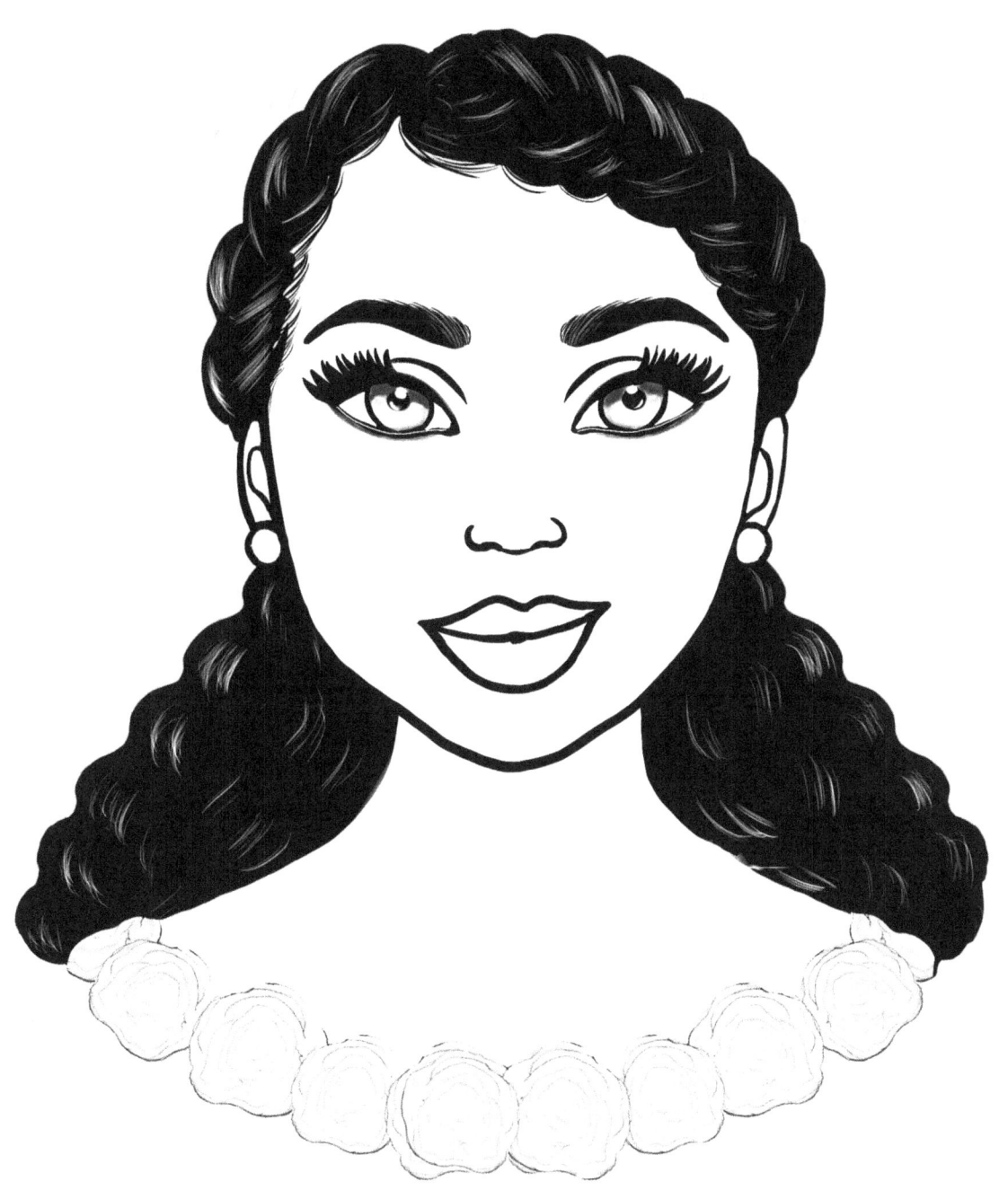

Fashionlistically Speaking

Choose Joy

Fashionlistically Speaking

But First, Coffee

Fashionlistically Speaking

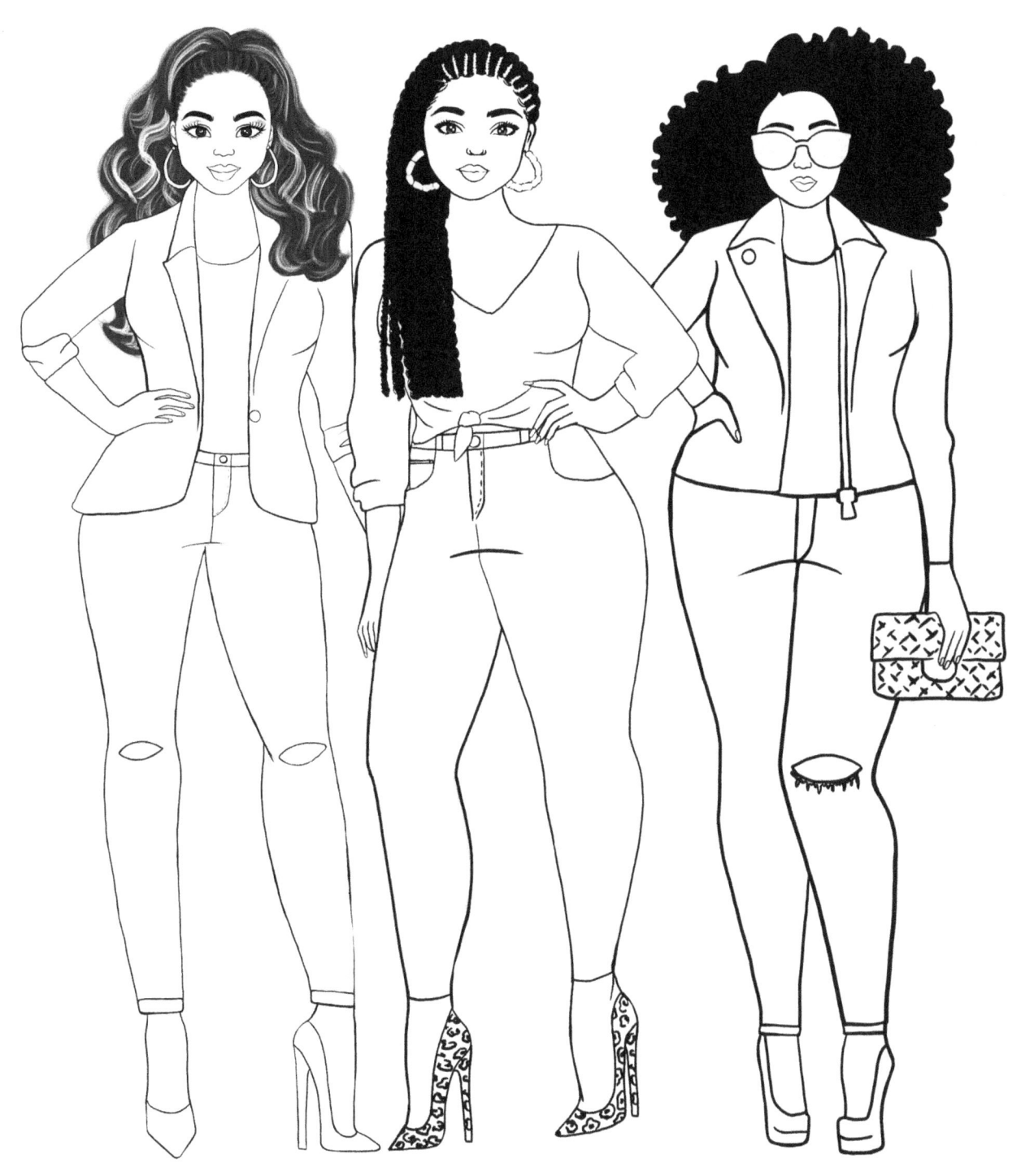

Fashionlistically Speaking

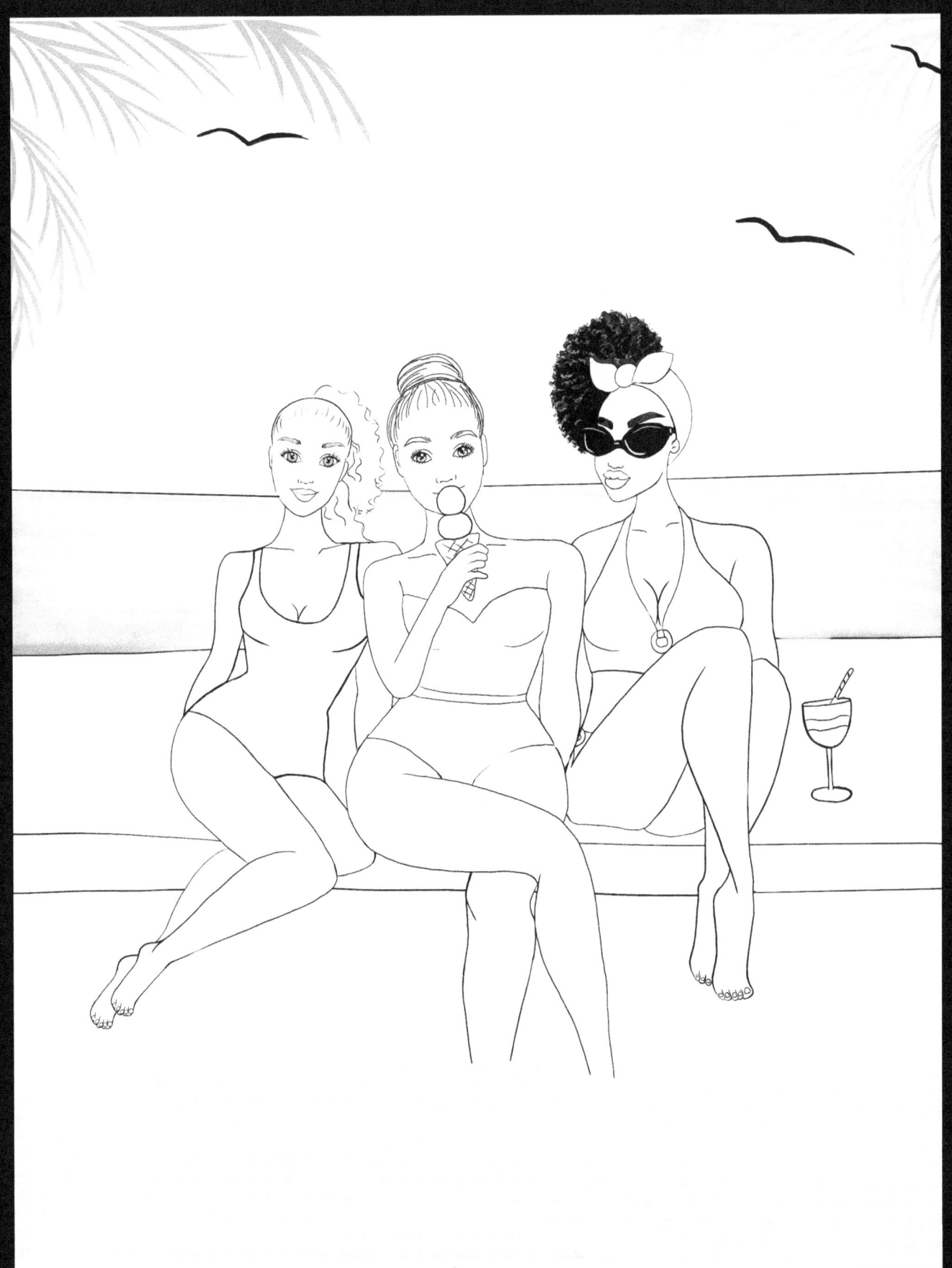

Fashionlistically Speaking

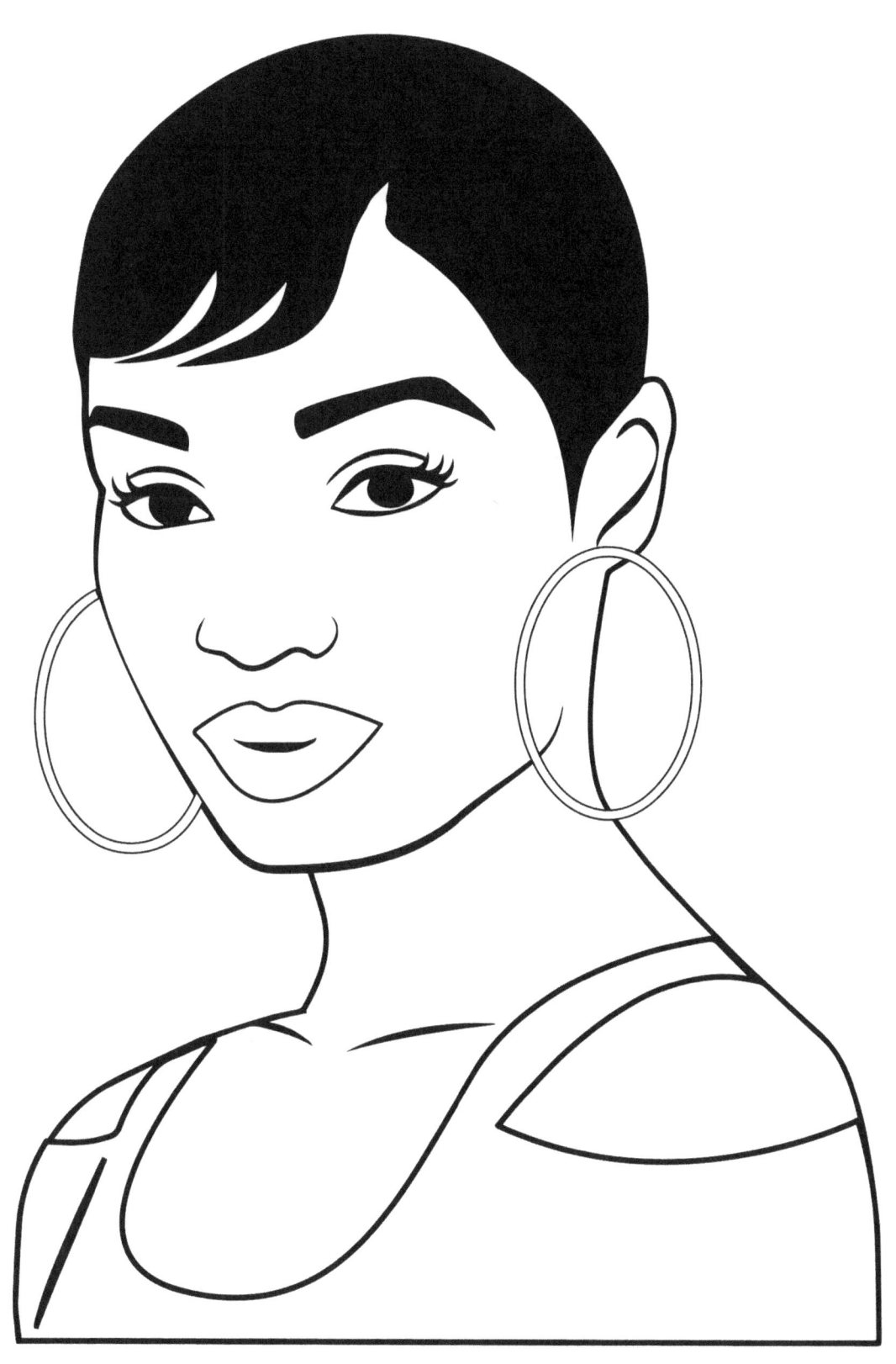

Fashionlistically Speaking

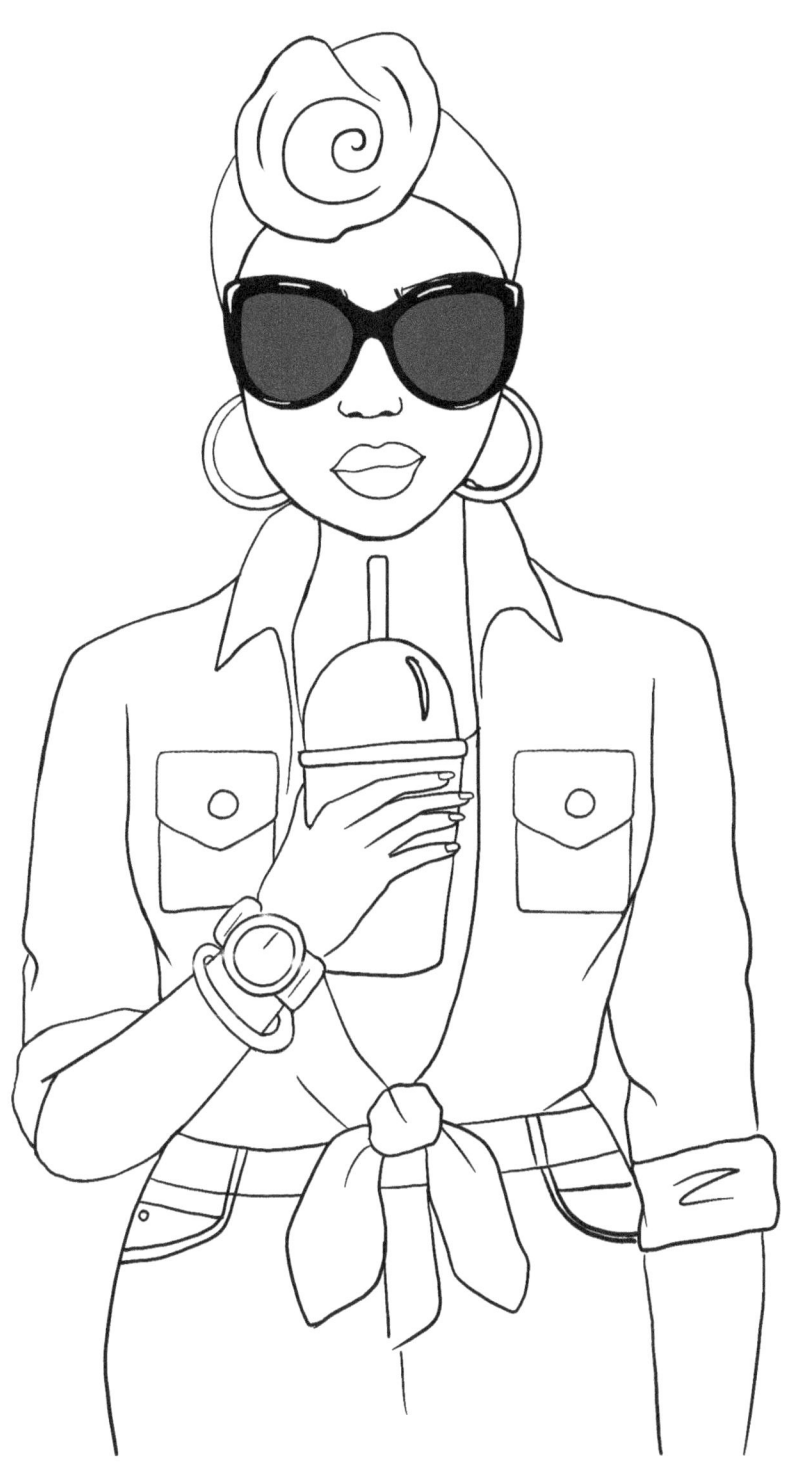

Fashionlistically Speaking

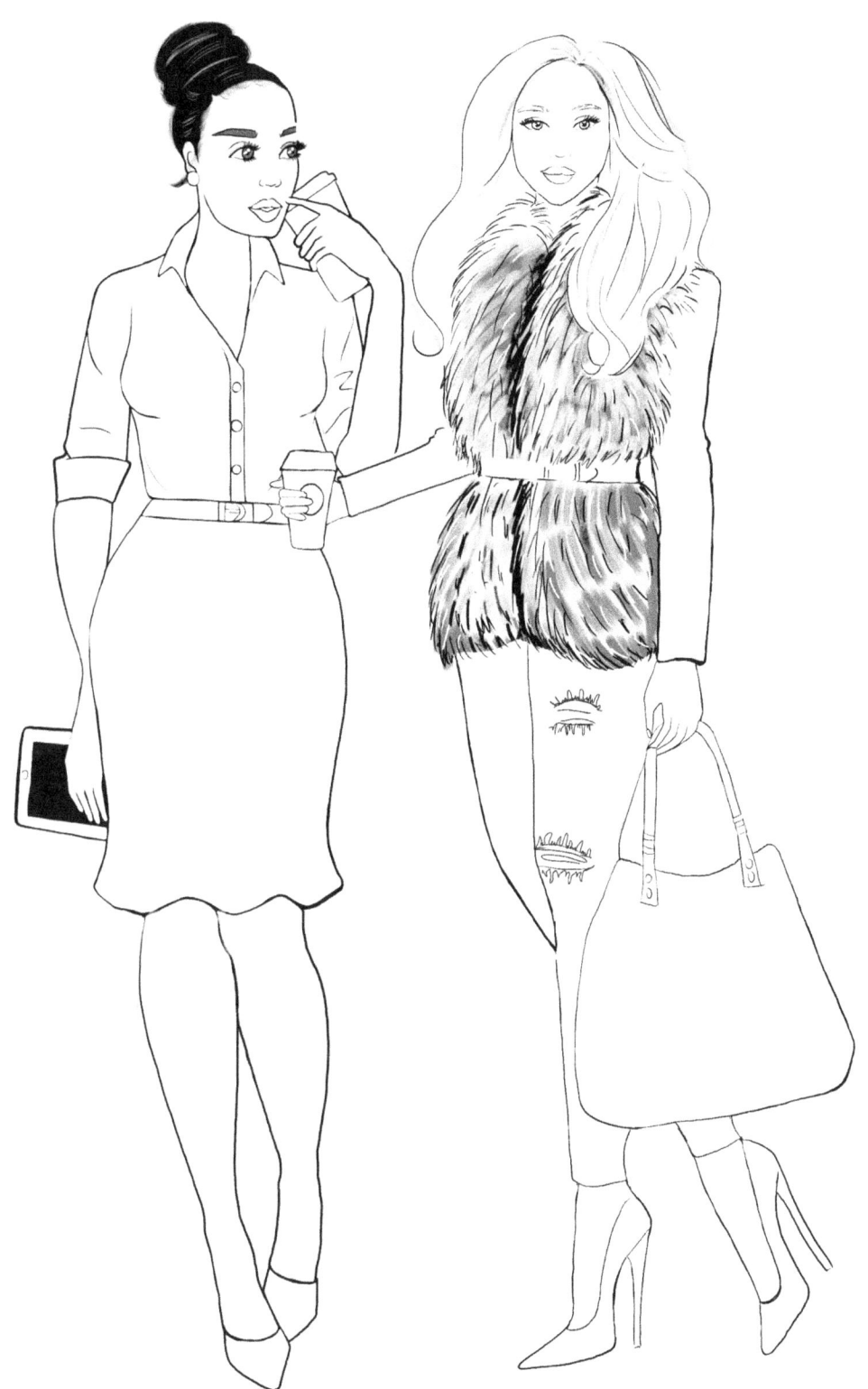

Fashionlistically Speaking

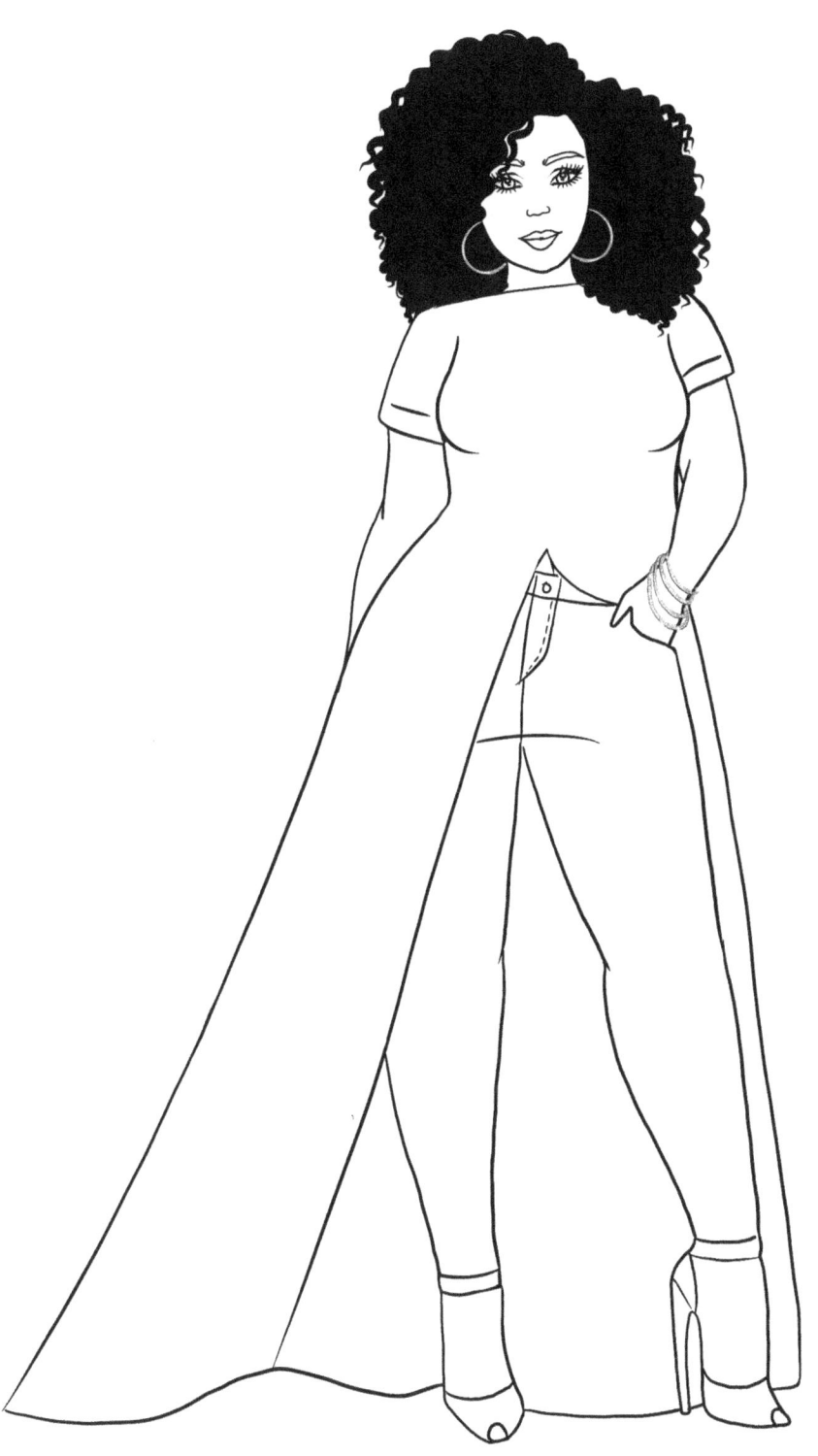

Fashionlistically Speaking

www.ingramcontent.com/pod-product-compliance
Lightning Source LLC
Chambersburg PA
CBHW080535220526
45465CB00006B/2717